CALLIGRAPHY PRACTICE WORKBOOK

Copyright © 2019

Disclaimer

All Rights Reserved. No part of this book may be reproduced or transmitted in any form or by any means, mechanical or electronic, including photocopying or recording, or by any information storage and retrieval system, or transmitted by email without permission in writing from the publisher. This book is for entertainment purposes only. The views expressed are those of the author alone.

This Book Belongs To

_____